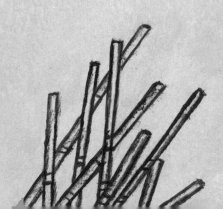

JUN

Gai See

What You Can See in Chinatown

by Roseanne Thong
illustrated by Yangsook Choi

Abrams Books for Young Readers
New York

Library of Congress Cataloging-in-Publication Data:
Thong, Roseanne.
   Gai see : what you can see in Chinatown / by Roseanne Thong ;
illustrated by Yangsook Choi.
       p. cm.
   Summary: In illustrations and rhyming text, depicts the vivid
sights, sounds, and smells of a Saturday morning outdoor
market in Chinatown.
   ISBN-13: 978-0-8109-9337-2
   ISBN-10: 0-8109-9337-6
  1. Chinese Americans—Juvenile fiction. [1. Chinese
Americans—Fiction. 2. Markets—Fiction. 3. Stories in rhyme.]
I. Choi, Yangsook, ill. II. Title.

PZ8.3.T328Wh 2007
[E]—dc22
                                    2006030437

Book design by Vivian Cheng

Published in 2007 by Abrams Books for Young Readers,
an imprint of Harry N. Abrams, Inc. All rights reserved.
No portion of this book may be reproduced, stored in a
retrieval system, or transmitted in any form or by any means,
mechanical, electronic, photocopying, recording, or otherwise,
without written permission from the publisher.

Printed and bound in China
10 9 8 7 6 5 4 3 2 1

HNA ■■■■■
harry n. abrams, inc.
a subsidiary of La Martinière Groupe
115 West 18th Street
New York, NY 10011
www.hnabooks.com

To Maya, who loves Chinese street markets
as much as I do, and to Nury, for bushels
of encouragement
—R.T.

To Seungdo and Youngae
—Y.C.

What in the world
could you possibly see
at an old *gai see*,
just you and me
on a warm and easy,
slightly breezy
springtime Saturday morning?

$2.⁰⁰
per Lb

薯仔
$1.⁰⁰

芋頭
$1.2⁰

Oodles of noodles,
fresh and dried—
try the ones with
egg inside.

Ramen, *cheong-fun*,
Shanghai styles
look like they
could stretch for miles!

A slipper store—
come take your pick—
with wooden clogs
that clack and click.

Velvet shoes
with pearls and beads
are just the ones
that sister needs!

What in the world
could you possibly see
at an old *gai see*
by a shady tree
on a hot and steamy,
melt ice-creamy
summery Sunday morning?

Tofu blocks
like soft white clay
or crispy squares
heaped on a tray.

Soybean milk
salty or sweet—
a nice, cool glass
sure beats the heat!

Bubbling tanks
of deep-sea fish,
just perfect for
your favorite dish.

Lobster, crab,
and slippery eel
dash and splash
as children squeal.

Mango, starfruit,
colors bright
glisten in the
morning light.

Dragon fruit
with scarlet scales,
lychees filling
woven pails.

楊
桃磚
$2.50

What in the world
could you possibly see
at an old *gai see*
beside the sea
on a cool and crispy,
windy, wispy
late-fall Friday morning?

Incense sticks
of red and gold
for worshiping
the gods of old.

Paper money
burned for prayer
to show ancestors
that we care.

A sweet shop with
round balls of dough—
our grandma's favorite,
long ago.

Chocolate coins
and sticky jellies,
just right for filling
little bellies.

Heaps of rice,
an egg that's fried,
and crispy roast duck
on the side.

A few short stools,
a tiny table—
use your chopsticks,
if you're able!

What in the world
could you possibly see
at an old *gai see*
where they serve hot tea
on a cold and freezing,
sniffling, sneezing
wintry Wednesday morning?

A store for
Chinese medicine
that's sure to make
you well again.

Tiny drawers of
herbs and seeds
for aches and pains
and other needs.

Choi sum, cabbage,
foot-long beans,
broccoli, peas,
and other greens.

Stacked in piles—
grab a bunch,
delicious for
your stir-fry lunch.

Money packets,
banners bright,
firecrackers
for the night.

Season's greetings
on the wall
say "Happy New Year"
to us all!

What in the world
could you possibly see
at an old *gai see*
where the smiles are free
on a warm and easy,
slightly breezy
any-season morning?

Glossary

Cheong-fun: Long, wide rice noodles that are often drenched in soy sauce. The name means "intestine noodle" in Chinese (they are long and wide like intestines).

Choi sum: A green leafy vegetable eaten stir-fried or steamed.

Dragon fruit: A large tropical fruit with layers of bright pink or red skin that look like scales. The inside has sweet, grayish-white flesh with black seeds that can be eaten.

Gai see: "Street market" in Cantonese. A lively place where vendors sell their goods, which are not easily found in the modern supermarket, from open-air stalls, on pushcarts, and in stores.

Incense sticks: Sticks—usually made of sandalwood—that give off a sweet-smelling smoke when burned. They are used for prayer and worship.

Money packets: Small red envelopes filled with "lucky money" given to children or unmarried adults during Chinese New Year.

Paper money: Paper traditionally burned as offerings for people who have died or to keep away ghosts.

Ramen: Long and wavy noodles like spaghetti that are usually precooked and sold with small packets of dried broth to make instant soup.

Shanghai noodles: Long, soft egg noodles that are fried with soy sauce and bits of chopped vegetables.

Songbirds: Birds often taken to restaurants—especially tea stalls—to accompany their owners as they eat. They are also taken out in cages for early-morning strolls.